D1328000

GERMANY AND EUROPE

A SPIRITUAL DISSENSION

GERMANY
AND EUROPE

A SPIRITUAL DISSENSION

BY

BENEDETTO CROCE

———

Translated and with an introduction by

VINCENT SHEEAN

RANDOM HOUSE · NEW YORK

FIRST PRINTING

THIS IS A WARTIME BOOK

The text is complete and unabridged,

but every effort has been made to comply with

the Government's request to conserve essential materials.

CONTENTS

———

Introduction:

Unnecessary for those who already know Croce's work

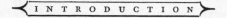

INTRODUCTION

Unnecessary for those

who already know Croce's work

BY VINCENT SHEEAN

CROCE's international reputation is great, but restricted. He does not speak plainly enough for plain people. It was never his intention to do so. Throughout a long life of scholarship in philosophy and history he has addressed himself primarily to other scholars, and secondarily to such members of the general public as have sufficiently acquired the habit of thought and are not averse to making an effort. Even in Italy, where his authority is felt most, his actual readers have been relatively few.

In translating these recent essays on a most contemporary subject I have often been tempted to break up his long sentences into shorter ones, to use, at times, a simpler language, and, in short, by the devices of professional experience, to reduce the philosopher into a journalist. This treason I have not committed. Where the actual genius of the English language is at variance with the genius of the Italian language another question arises: sometimes English does not tolerate certain grammatical structures, rejects whole parts of speech and takes a different sort of flight of its own. The English

3

and Italian languages are not at all harmonious with regard to their adverbs; some Italian adverbs have so many possible English translations that the picking and choosing among them becomes a task of much delicacy. In another translation I made some years ago of a French book, I had to operate upon the tenses: the book was written in the historical present throughout, and I had to put it all in the past—which, with compound tenses, developed such complexities that even in that simple text there arose some doubt in my mind over my fidelity to the original. In this case the difficulty has been in thought as well as in syntax or style, and its resolution has been to leave Croce's thought and expression most respectfully in the form native to him, only transposing or altering in the instances where English and Italian cannot agree.

2

Benedetto Croce was born at Pescasseroli in the province of Aquila on February 25, 1866. His family came from Abruzzo, but was transferred by his grandfather to Naples. He received a Catholic education, and would appear to have arrived at philosophy through theology—the classic route for an Italian. It would be an error, I think, to classify him crudely as an "atheist"—as the popular *Story of Philosophy*, by Mr. Will Durant, has not hesitated to do—since his work contradicts any such idea. If the reader would read and re-read the opening page and a half of the fourth essay in this little volume (on "Duties and Duty") he will discern the error clearly enough.

In 1883, when Croce was seventeen, his parents and a sister were killed in an earthquake at Casamicciola. He was himself buried in the ruins of the house for hours, and it was some years before his health was fully restored. After this catastrophe he went to live in Rome with his uncle, Silvio Spaventa, who had become his guardian. Spaventa was one of those remarkable men of the old Italian Right, along with Ricàsoli, Lanza, Quintino Sella and others, to whom Croce has frequently paid tribute for their courage and honor, even though his own ideas very soon began a journey which was to lead him far away from theirs. While he was in Rome Croce entered the university, but did not pursue his studies there long; in 1886, when he was twenty, he returned to Naples and began those local researches which resulted in his enchanting early books on the past of the place.

His first work in print was published when he was twenty-two. It was *Luisa Sanfelice e la Congiura dei Baccher* (printed at Trani), an account of that unhappy lady who became, all unwittingly, a heroine to the Neapolitan revolutionaries in 1799 and was beheaded after the Bourbon restoration. Croce's sound and serious methods of research gave solidity to the old stories; he examined every document, every church or house or stone, which might contribute to the reconstruction of the past; he was able to talk to old men who could repeat the local traditions. Thus all his early work on Neapolitan legend and history has a character quite unique in that field—for it is rare that such gifts as his are so employed.

He studied the Neapolitan theatre from the Renaissance to the end of the eighteenth century for his book *I Teatri di Napoli* (1888), and when we read it now we wonder at the erudition, industry and patience of a man so young—a man who, moreover, was already immersed in philosophical study and preparation. His love of Naples, his connection with the stones of the place and the voices of the people, started him out in a vein to which he has returned again and again, and could return today if he were so inclined—that of patient and tender research into every detail of the local past.

Meanwhile German philosophy had become a ruling interest, even though he was writing about something else. He had attended the lectures of Labriola in the University of Rome—Antonio Labriola, the first Italian Marxist of any intellectual pretension. Labriola was a philosopher, at first Hegelian and then anti-Hegelian, who declared himself a "radical" in 1885 and made his discovery of Marx in 1890. He engaged in a correspondence with Friedrich Engels and the other German survivors and disciples of the Marxian epos. According to Croce, Labriola's course in the philosophy of history at the University of Rome thereafter became a straightforward exposition of the principles of historic materialism. (Croce had himself attended these lectures before the Marxian revelation.) Probably under the influence of Labriola, who was at that time firing the minds of all the young with his Marxian enthusiasm, Croce carried out in the 1890's a thoroughgoing philosophical examination and criticism of the Marxian doctrine of history. The essays he wrote on the subject were published in his book on historic materialism (*Materialismo storico ed economia marxistica*, 1900). In effect, he rejects Marx's determinism and subjects parts of the economic doctrine (the theory of surplus value, for instance) to destructive criticism. At the same time it is easy to see, and it is confirmed in all his later work, what an immense revitalizing influence he perceives in the advent of Marxism to the intellectual life of Europe. In his *History of Italy from 1871 to 1914*, published twenty-six years later, he pays tribute to Labriola and to all the first Italian translators and followers of Marx, who brought new life into Italian thought. After the heroic period of the unification of Italy had ended in a bourgeois liberal monarchy, in which the main interest of events lay in the balancing of the budget, the young and the restless were inclined to say, "What is the good of this?" The anticlimax of success was upon them. The professors had little to offer, and the young were obeying the law of their nature in demanding something more. Stagnation, sterility and pessimism were or seemed to be the only results brought to Italy by her wild fight for freedom and unity. Into this stagnation came the Marxian system with its absolute assurance of social progress by revolution, its bitter and irrefutable analysis of capitalism, its whole fearless assumption of the burden of history and society. Young and active minds came to life again; and although Croce rejects materialism, and his own whole philosophy is an anti-materialist structure, he accepts it eclectically, as part of historic progress, as something historically necessary. His view of Christianity in another stage of society is not dissimilar. If I have not totally misunderstood him, his attitude toward Marx is rather like that of Voltaire toward God: If Marx had not existed it would have been necessary to invent him.

The formulation of Croce's own philosophy and its publication in parts occupied all the first decade of the present century. The work as a whole bears the name *Philosophy of the Spirit* (*La Filosofia dello Spirito*). It is divided into four parts: Aesthetic, Logic, Philosophy of Conduct (Ethics and Economics), and Theory and History of Historiography; publication was completed by 1910. I do not feel myself possessed of enough philosophical training to attempt a summary of this philosophy, nor have I sufficiently studied the basic work of the master. I shall therefore reprint part of the summary given in the *Encyclopaedia Britannica*, XIV edition, Vol. 6, page 732.[1] This was written by John Alexander Smith, Waynflete Professor of Moral and Metaphysical Philosophy, Oxford, 1910-36.

The philosophy of Croce, often erroneously classed as "Hegelian," had its avowed sources in the ideas underlying the literary criticism of Francesco de Sanctis, and, more generally and remotely, in those adumbrated in the Scienza Nuova *of G. B. Vico, both, like himself, Neapolitans. More significantly, it arises from and perpetually returns to his own personal experience in his lifelong and multifarious activity as a student of literature and history. Here he finds himself in vital touch with concrete reality, and deliberately confines his reflections to the content of actual or enacted history with a view to its interpretation. Hence he has been led to assert the identity of concrete philosophy with history, and to define the task of abstract philosophy as the discovery and formulation of the immanent methodology of history. From the common domain of both he excludes any supposed realities which transcend experience, and abstains from speculations about such, as he also does about primal origins and ultimate ends. History as enacted and occurring and history as interpreting what is thus "given" he views as the work of one Spirit, which there expresses and embodies itself. In every part and moment of history that Spirit is wholly and indivisibly present and active. Its presence and operation are not confined to human history, but extend in all directions to the utmost bounds of experience. The Spirit which is thus omnipresent throughout the whole content of experience is indivisibly one, but its unity is also a quaternity, and it has in its structure four eternally distinct and distinguishable "grades," the ordered circle of which in its life or progress it perpetually traverses, so endowing or fulfilling itself with experience and ever enriching its*

---

[1] Quoted by permission of the *Encyclopaedia Britannica*.

being. Its four functions in their conjoint exercise generate the contents of experience, within which we can and must distinguish four corresponding grades, stages, kinds or realms, the respective subject-matters of aesthetic, logical, economic and ethical theory, departments of philosophy, which together without addition constitute the whole of it.

In its total cognitive function this Spirit manifests itself as art, the first or "dawn" form of knowledge. In this grade it expresses itself in individual embodiments; in so expressing itself it at once creates and beholds what it creates, and has for its objects (which are also its works) whatsoever in experience presents a characteristic individuality. In its second cognitive stage, as logic or abstract philosophy, it expresses, brings to existence and view, and so knows whatsoever is universal. Uniting, as it cannot but do, both functions, and thus becoming concrete in history, it effects an a priori synthesis between what is individual and what is universal; in doing so, it wins actual understanding of the real and enters upon a course of knowledge which runs from sense-perception up to explicit history. The history which thus comes to be understood is wholly the work of the same Spirit in the exercise of its total practical function, which has two corresponding grades, in the lower or earlier of which it enacts what is individual, in the higher or later what is universal, or, rather again, in its actual or concrete exercise, enacts both in one, and so fills the stage of history with its deeds. Still more actually or concretely, it is active at once as making or creating and as knowing or understanding its own history, which is its whole self. The only reality which can truly be called absolute is a history without beginning and without end, self-begotten and self-explaining.

The article in the *Encyclopaedia* concludes with the statement that this system seems, for many, already to occupy a position in the world of contemporary philosophy comparable to that occupied in the nineteenth century by the system of Hegel.

Without attempting to add anything analytical or expository to what is so well said above by better authority, I should like to state the reasons why this philosophy strongly attracts and fascinates me. I came to it late, having already been through several attempts to believe the systems of other masters. It always seemed to me that in the parts of their work which I was able to understand and which most intimately concerned me—that is, the life, work and destiny of mankind—too much of the possible was ruled out. The system of Marx does not allow for numerous discoveries that have already been made in psychology, anthropology, biological chemistry and other sciences. Simple materialism is even contradicted by some more easily observable ordinary phenomena in politics and society. Hegel presents the vast contradiction of a philosophy of history which culminates in the nineteenth-century Prussian state. Until I encountered the work of Croce I never had acquaintance with a modern philosophical or philosophico-historical system which gave enough leeway for the infinite possibilities of nature; which, without teleological aberrations, dogma or religiosity, permitted the human spirit to exist in nature; and which, in its concrete application to the various historical periods and places studied by Croce himself, seemed to relate man and his life on this planet to a grand natural design of harmonious progression, which, whether it fully and actually exists or not, is at least provided for, or not ruled out, by the system itself.

3

Croce's work after 1910 consisted of the application of his system to a variety of subjects in literature and history. His study of *Vico* appeared in 1911; his *Goethe* in 1919; his *Dante* in 1920. *Ariosto, Shakespeare e Corneille* came out the same year. *Poesia e non poesia*, an Oxford lecture, appeared in 1923. His *Storia del Regno di Napoli*, a return to the local past which had never ceased to interest him, was published in 1925, the *Storia d'Italia dal 1871 al 1915* appeared in 1928, the *Storia dell'età barocca in Italia* in 1929, *Manzoni* in 1930. The *Storia d'Europa nel secolo decimonono*, a sort of historico-philosophical hymn to liberty, came out in 1932.

Aside from all these and other books written as books, Croce throughout this century has been indefatigable and prolific in smaller forms. He founded the review called *La Critica* in 1903 and never ceased to publish it, even in the midst of Fascism and war. It was his good fortune to encounter a publisher who understood his purposes and was willing to do his part—against many difficulties—in carrying them out. No serious subject is too small for Croce to investigate; no subject is too large to be briefly considered; nothing in art, literature or history is beyond his range, with one exception, which is music. (In his *History of Italy from 1871 to 1915*, otherwise of unique value for the comprehension of Italy's development, the name of Giuseppe Verdi does not once occur.) In *La Critica* for these past forty years the philosopher has treated a huge number of subjects with unfailing virtuosity. Often it is on these small specific themes—a street corner in Naples, a bandit legend in the hills—that the Philosophy of the Spirit comes out at us with most force.

Croce has no literary conventionality whatsoever. The choice of theme matters little, since practically everything interests him; what governs and informs it all is the Philosophy of the Spirit, and each separate study is an expression of that system of which he deeply feels himself to be a part as

well as the creator. His independence of external circum-
stance is due, of course, to financial security; he has never
had to worry about money—his forebears did that; he has
never had too much or too little, but always enough.

After the formulation of the Philosophy of the Spirit
(completed in 1910) Croce's position became very great in
Italian intellectual life. It is now pre-eminent. A man without much formal academic training himself, who has shown
himself at various times sharply critical of academic states
of mind and habit, he nevertheless exercises great power over
the universities. The University of Naples, indeed, is practically his; its rector, Adolfo Omodeo, is one of those disciples
of Croce who have in their own work applied the Philosophy
of the Spirit to specific historical subjects. (He became Minister of Education on April 21, 1944.) Omodeo's study of
De Maistre (*Un reazionario*, 1935-1936) was published originally in *La Critica* and, although stylistically very different,
is informed by the spirit of Croce. Omodeo's main investiga-
tion has been in Christian origins, and has involved him in
exegetical scholarship which would appear to be far from
Croce's realm—nor would Croce ever have explored a subject
so tangential to the main course of life as the mysticism of
St. John the Evangelist—yet this extension of method is itself a part of the system, and actually demanded by it.

Politicians, too, became aware of the Neapolitan master
in due course. With his philosophical system Croce must,
of course, take a deep interest in concrete or enacted history,
whether it is of the present moment or any other; consequently the political, social and economic environment in
which the philosophy was evolved becomes at once a part of
it and a subject to which it must be applied. How much

Giolitti understood of all this we take leave to doubt, but at any rate he was aware that the Liberal party in Italy had in Croce a distinguished ornament. It was no doubt through his advice that Croce was made a Senator of the Kingdom in 1910 (although at the precise moment of the nomination Giolitti was no longer in office). A Senator of the Kingdom is appointed for life, and consequently Croce was a Senator all through the period of the Fascist mania.

At the outbreak of the war of 1914-1918 Croce, as Senator and as philosopher, deplored it and wished to see Italy stay out of it. He regarded it as an economic conflict between imperialisms—the point of view of many great men throughout the world, rejected by the masses. When Italy entered the war he followed the course of the conflict with all the natural emotional patriotism of an Italian citizen, as he explains in the first of these four essays. At the end of the war he tried to use his influence in the direction of the earliest possible restoration of general European culture and harmony, and was in a position to do something about it, since Giolitti had called him to office as Minister of Public Instruction.

The fifth Giolitti cabinet was formed on June 15, 1920, and lasted a little over one year. During that year the disorders which encouraged the growth of Fascism were taking place; Giolitti, for whatever reason, seemed willing to permit the Socialists on one side and the Fascists on the other to try almost any experiment in violence. In foreign affairs the principal question was that of the Adriatic, which had been exacerbated and made almost impossible of solution by the histrionics of Gabriele d'Annunzio. Giolitti supported his foreign minister, Carlo Sforza, in a very unpopular but necessary compromise with the Yugoslavs which was formulated in the Treaty of Rapallo (November 22, 1920) and became a part of the European fundament until 1939.

Croce no doubt regarded all these occurrences with keen interest, but I think the main event of 1920 for him was the commemoration of the sixth centenary of the death of Dante (November 17, 1920). In the biographical sketch prepared by himself for the Italian Who's Who, this is the only event of his public life which he mentions.

Then came Fascism. At the very outset it appears that Croce did not oppose it; perhaps he did not understand it; in any case he seems to have thought of it as a mass movement, and any mass movement was preferable to stagnation and sterility. As its nature and intentions became clear he rapidly moved into the position of an unshakable opponent, where he remained throughout its fantastic career, watching it from his study windows with the frozen contempt of a man who sees fools outdoing themselves, but also with the bitter and terrible suffering of a man who sees his beloved country commit suicide.

He returned to his philosophy, and it sustained him. During those years he must daily have been thankful to Dante, to Goethe, to all the familiars of his mind for their kindred assurances down the centuries. The external world, too, sent signals of solidarity from time to time. Hardly anybody with a trace of intellectual interest during those years could visit Naples without going to see him, to get some word of the Italy that was and will be. Italians from the universities frequented his house; it was a sort of place of pilgrimage. The Fascists railed against him; some young hoodlums once broke in and would have attacked the philosopher but for the furious intervention of Signora Croce; he was subjected to the most constant surveillance and many threats. In effect he was a prisoner of that house for almost twenty years. But he was protected by a prestige so great that Mussolini could never make up his mind to imprison him. He also had the collaboration of a singularly devoted publisher, Giuseppe Laterza of Bari, who continued to publish Croce's work, against every difficulty imaginable, throughout the period. The *History of Italy from 1871 to 1915* and the *History of Europe in the Nineteenth Century*, two books which are the Philosophy of the Spirit beautifully applied to concrete and enacted history, came out in the era of Fascist triumph and were nevertheless read.

The chief reason why Croce was not suppressed, killed or imprisoned probably is to be found in the fact that the Fascists, illiterate or ill-educated people for the most part, could not understand him. Some no doubt did. Mussolini, in the days when he could still read, probably read some of Croce's work and decided that it was too "academic" to matter. Undoubtedly he also had a sense of the prestige of Croce even though he did not understand it. (He had the same feeling about Toscanini, and was infuriated by the behavior of the Fascist hoodlums toward him.) Whatever the reason, Croce wrote and Laterza published throughout the Fascist era, and although they had many difficulties, the fifty volumes are there, deposited upon the mind of the world.

When Mussolini fell on July 25, 1943, Croce's position changed at once. From being a prisoner in his own house, to which only the very courageous could go, he became a sort of oracle. Italy, bewildered and suffering, looked at him from the ruins and asked for a word. He had written all the words already; he was the one man who had known, with absolute certainty, that the Fascist mania would end in this horrible disaster; he had always known it because of philosophy and history. In this moment what more could he say to them?

He said a few simple things. He told his own party (the Liberals) and the five other parties which possess organizations and leaders that it would be a meaningless falsification or worse to take office under a King who is indissolubly associated in every Italian mind with Fascism. He told them that he, personally, could not support any economic program because he felt no assurance that circumstances would permit a program to be executed, and he did not wish to give false promises, like a politician. He said truth, freedom and justice were the aim, and anything more specific (such as the nationalization of banks, the agrarian reform, etc., etc.) should be advocated by those who felt that it might be possible to enact the idea. Consequently he remains a Liberal, the leader of a small party with principles but no concrete program. Most of the anti-Fascist youth which is devoted to Croce has passed over into the Partito d'Azione, which proposes to adopt and carry out a social and economic program of a specific nature applying, within the limits set by human frailty, the august and abstract principles of freedom. There is no conflict here: the Partito d'Azione is merely concretely applying, in whatever ways it can find, the principles of Croce—in association with the Socialists and Communists who are attempting to give concrete enactments of other ideas.

The political position of Croce is therefore simply Socratic. He will answer anybody's questions, but he cannot take a public position in practical politics because his eclecticism in philosophy prevents any form of partisanship. He was anti-Fascist because Fascism was anti-historical, was an attempt to violate the laws of history and philosophy. The ruin which it brought upon Italy is felt by nobody more strongly than by Croce, but he knows in his soul that he is not a practical politician and cannot, at the age of seventy-eight, suddenly become one.

On April 21, 1944, after King Victor Emmanuel II had made a formal public promise to retire as soon as Rome should be taken again from the Germans, the Italian anti-Fascist parties agreed to form a government under Marshal Badoglio and pressed upon Croce the necessity of entering that united cabinet as a Minister of State without portfolio—a purely consultative function which does not greatly change his status.

He is the most eminent living Italian, and therefore has an obligation, which he acknowledges, to receive all those who come to him and to give them such answers as he can find to their questions. He is even willing to allow his immense spiritual authority to be used for practical political ends, but actually to participate in the turmoil of affairs is, I think, beyond his nature and outside his purposes.

Physically he has not had to endure anything more serious than a rather robust old age during the war. When the bombing of Naples made it advisable to leave his house in the Via Trinità Maggiore, Signora Croce found a house at Sorrento where they now live. This house, which used to belong to the Astor family in New York (and perhaps still does), is large and comfortable, although very cold in winter. Croce's house and library in Naples lost some windows in the bombings, but are otherwise intact, although the exquisite cloister

of Santa Chiara nearby is now in ruins. When our invasion
began to creep up toward Sorrento and the Germans moved
to meet it, the British Navy—greatly to its credit—made a
dash across from Capri to rescue the philosopher. He went
with his daughter Elena and her husband, Raimondo Craveri, as it was considered that the Germans would probably
shoot him. Signora Croce, careful of her house as always,
remained at Sorrento with the other daughters, and the
Germans did not disturb them.

After the events of September and October, 1943, Croce's
former colleague, Count Carlo Sforza, returned to Italy from
a long exile abroad and associated himself with Croce in the
group of political leaders. He became a Minister of State on
April 21, 1944. Sforza is a man of the world, with a fluency,
elegance and urbanity which do not seem to consort particularly well with the philosopher's drastic personality, and yet
they remain in agreement on the important immediate
points. Perhaps Croce feels that for practical politics Count
Sforza has gifts and experience which Italy now needs; at any
rate Sforza's voice has always been on the right side, and it
is such voices that should now be heard.

Croce is a doctor *honoris causa* of the universities of Oxford and Freiburg, President of the Royal (Italian) Academy
of Moral and Political Science, and a member of the Prussian
Academy. He is married and has four daughters.

4

In the summer of 1934 I was living in a village on Lago
Maggiore, finishing my book *Personal History*. This was an
attempt to relate an individual to the general life by an

account of those experiences (and only those) which concerned the general experience. It was intended to be both personal and a history. I had never read Croce at the time, and had no idea that there was a philosophical system in existence which might have given me light on my way. Among the Italian books I read during the summer (and I read chiefly Italian books because no others were obtainable in the villages roundabout) was Pietro Colletta's *Storia del Reame di Napoli*. This is a rather crabbed but beautiful work, written with the inherited Latinity and compression which sometimes occur in non-literary Italian; Colletta was a general who had served the revolutionary (or at least national) cause in Naples against the Austrians and his book was written in prison. In it there occur some sentences about the story of Luisa Sanfelice, who became a heroine to the Neapolitan revolution of 1799 through an unlucky love, and for it died afterwards on the scaffold.

This story captivated my imagination in some way. I knew nothing more about it than those references in Colletta's book; no other books on the subject could be found where I was. The sentence that particularly held me, and holds me still, was this: *"fu rea, se rea fu, soltanto d'amore."* She was guilty, if she was guilty, only of love.

After visits to London and New York I repaired to Naples to find out what I could about this story, since there were elements in the whole social and political scene against which it took place which also attracted me. As soon as I got to Naples I discovered that the best book on the subject was by Croce. I read it and then began to read everything else of his on related subjects that I could find. In my boarding-house on the Via Caracciolo there was a professor of eco-

nomics from the University of Bari. He took me to friends
who took me to Croce.

At the time I did not realize that the subject in which I
was interested was also the subject which had aroused his
first piece of writing. (I only discovered this in 1944.) At
the time I was rather intimidated by the whole procedure:
the vast house with its almost invisible ceilings, the immense
library, the circle of disciples who sat waiting for the master
to speak. Croce came and went at will, paying little attention
to whoever might be in the room. (I understood that sometimes people gathered there and waited and he never appeared at all if he was busy at something else.) Everybody
had come for a different reason, but all because, whatever
the subject, they hoped for a word from him about it. I think
I had some glimmer then of the power of wisdom—that it
was something everybody wanted, hoped for, would attend
upon, whatever the conditions. When my friend explained
to Croce what I was working upon he became interested and
even voluble (for him). He asked me if I had investigated
the character of Carlo Lauberg, a very curious revolutionary
of 1799. I said not particularly, beyond the references in the
books I had read. Croce had himself written a monograph
on this personage some years before and published it in
La Critica. He now arose and began to climb ladders. The
shelves of his library stretched to a great height and the
monograph he wished to find was at the very top of the room.
(Nobody but Croce knew then or knows now where each
book in this vast library is.) He climbed while I shivered.
But he did not fall. He came back down the ladder and
dusted off the monograph and came over and gave it to me.
Immediately thereafter he started to talk on a different sub-

ject with some Neapolitan scholar (I believe it was Michel-angelo Schipa) and I was finished for that day.

Afterwards I returned to the house. Sometimes we sat in that rather arid room where the clients were accustomed to gather; at other times, when there happened to be no clients or the Senator did not wish to see them, we sat in his small study. At the instigation of our mutual friend I gave him a copy of my book, *Personal History*, never expecting him to read it. He read it and found interest in it. I now realize that this is because in some rather inexplicable way, from another world and emotionally rather than intellectually, it connected with his system. (I am not making claims; I am only trying to tell the truth.) There occurred an incident which no doubt he has forgotten; it was related to me by our mutual friend. An art critic of renown and bad character came into the study and saw Croce with my book at hand. (The mutual friend and Signora Croce were both present.) The celebrated art critic said with his accustomed peevishness: "Why are you reading that journalistic rubbish?" Croce replied severely: "It is not rubbish. It has something to do with history."

In the years that passed afterwards I neither saw nor communicated with him. I continued to read his work when I could; there were months when I read nothing else while I was writing the novel about Luisa Sanfelice. (The novel had an astonishing success in the Italian translation, incidentally, even though the Fascists had so truncated it that none of the ideas and none of the implications were left—only the bare story which they could have got out of the encyclopaedia.) Sometimes I heard that he was in grave trouble, and at other times that he was seriously ill. I have never at any moment ceased to be conscious of him as the inheritor of the Italian past and as one great pulse in the universal mind. No such truly European spirit has ever existed for me, that is to say in my own personal life. He has always seemed to me to be of the company of Dante and Shakespeare, even though his poetry is in philosophy and history, and therefore will not strike upon so many minds or leave such echoes in the air.

When we invaded Italy in September, I was a lieutenant-colonel in the United States Army Air Forces, as I still am. I had certain well-defined functions in the Salerno operation and carried them out as best I could. It was no part of my duty to go and see Croce, and so I did not. I worried about him a good deal (there was one moment when we were told the Germans had carried him off to the north and shot him). Then I ran into some of my former colleagues, the newspaper correspondents, who told me they had seen him alive and well at Capri.

On October 13th I was transferred to the Tactical Air Force on the Adriatic side of the peninsula, and discovered the bookshop of the Laterza brothers in Bari. These brothers, Franco and Nino, were the sons and heirs of Croce's friend, Giuseppe Laterza, who had died shortly after the downfall of Mussolini. I began to frequent their bookshop and, one thing leading to another, we became friends. Throughout this past winter I spent as much time as I could with them (Sunday lunch practically always) and we talked a great deal of Croce. One Sunday Croce's son-in-law (Elena's husband) appeared: Raimondo Craveri. I found in him a very sharp and active mind, grave misgivings, serious preoccupations. I had been reading Croce again and had fallen upon an essay he wrote in 1936 on the German problem called *La Germania che abbiamo amata*. I asked Mondo if he would ask Croce, on his return to the other side, if I might be allowed to translate this for some American periodical, as I thought it had some light to shed for those who know light when they see it.

I do not relate all this out of sheer triviality, but merely to show how this little book occurred.

Craveri went back to Sorrento and apparently set Croce to considering the subject. At the New Year I had to go to the other side for business of the Tactical Air Force; meeting Raimondo and Elena in Naples, I went with them to Positano and Sorrento.

When we went into the room Signora Croce was building a fire and the philosopher was talking to two of his clients. Even though the house was different—almost in the sea; nothing but the sea to be seen from the windows—this was at once familiar; it was like the Via Trinità Maggiore.

Croce and I talked, as I remember, almost entirely about the evil eye and various charms against it. At one moment he darted across the room to the catalogue of his library. (He had been allowed to bring only ten thousand volumes to Sorrento and has subsequently complained repeatedly, "How can one live without books?" But he had his catalogue.) In this catalogue he searched for a while until he found the best book that had ever been written about the evil eye. It was in English, by a man named Ellsworthy, and was published in London in 1896.

At one point he gave me the typewritten text of the first essay in this volume and said he wanted to put three others with it and have it translated into English. As he moved about the room he picked up and put together, from the desk and the shelves and the files, the four essays and the epigraph which compose the book. One (the first) had been especially written for this purpose; one (*La Germania che abbiamo amata*) dates from 1936 and is the one I had originally asked to translate; the other two were written at the beginning of this last winter. The epigraph at the end was composed to be cut in a tombstone over the twenty-three men, women and children killed by the Germans near the village of Caiazzo.

I am sensible of the honor he does me in permitting this translation. The book is small but it is not slight; there are mighty things in it; it is the thought and feeling of an erudite, passionate and dedicated spirit. The dedication is to humanity. There is very little hope that the German problem, complex and obscured by a tangle of hatreds, will be solved in such a spirit, especially since there are so few men of power and position who feel in this way or are willing even to read philosophical thought about concrete history. Still, for what it may bring, here is what Croce has written on this subject.

Confessions of an Italian "Germanophile"
who cannot discover within himself in this respect
anything for which he should repent

Confessions of an Italian "Germanophile"

who cannot discover within himself in this respect

anything for which he should repent

"GERMANOPHILE" (like "Anglophile" and "Francophile" and similar expressions) cannot be said except in reference to something which is objectively prized and is the consensus of concepts, tendencies and moral ideals, of institutions and customs, of political intentions; so true is this that with the formation of such consensi such love is set alight, varies with their variation, and is spent when they weaken or fail. There could be no different origin except one strangely imaginative and pathological, such as I observed in my adolescence in a worthy priest, a most excellent Latinist, who was enamored, actually with melting sweetness and sighs of love—guess of whom?—of the island of Malta, which, for that matter, he had never visited or thought of visiting.

And I was "Germanophile," or was so called, chiefly because I insisted upon holding in high esteem the thought and methodicity of German studies: which was nothing more than the recognition of an historic fact, that is of the powerful impulse which German thinkers and scholars, during the last years of the eighteenth and the first decades of the nineteenth century, had, more than any other European people, given to philosophy and philology, carrying forward, for the matter of that, the preceding work of other countries in Europe, and above all of Italy. And the result I deduced from this was that it would not be legitimate to ignore or neglect an acquisition of such great value. In this I was only following the recommendation and example given in other days by our men of the Risorgimento, who, precisely when they were fighting the German domination in Italy, placed themselves voluntarily in the school of its philosophical and historiographical thought,[1] holding back those ingenuous nationalists (who were furthermore almost all lazy or unintelligent) who demanded that the limpid Italian brain should abhor "Teutonic mists"—which is to say, in other terms, that they wished to forbid it that new matter upon which it could exercise its gifts of limpidity.

In fact this was the question; not of an impossible passive acceptance, but of the possible and active acceptance which is in the act itself correction, collaboration and further progress. In truth, I have always smiled at the qualification of "Hegelian" which has been pinned on me, not only because logically there should have been added the qualificatory adjectives of all the other thinkers I had likewise studied (not content with being, as Goethe said, *ein Narr auf eigne Hand*, a fool on his own hook), but also because I perceived the

---

[1] See the essay on "German Culture in Italy in the Age of the Risorgimento" (in *Uomini e Cose della vecchia Italia*, Bari, 1943, II, 355-67). I give notice that, as in the case of other references I shall make in footnotes, these are necessities of documentation and not invitations to read such works of mine. (B.C.)
Uomini e Cose della vecchia Italia has not been translated into English. (Tr.)

motive of such a qualification in the mental habit of "classifying," of putting into some sort of pigeonhole, which is supposed to be already known, judged and condemned, all writers, so as to get rid of them and throw off the fatigue of having to understand them. The truth is that I soon became aware of the vice of Hegel, and in general of the German philosophers of his period, which was that of crushing and distorting beneath the weight of an enormous metaphysical superposition their thoughts of genius, which it was necessary to pull out of that pressure, refreshing and revivifying them and letting them work in the new thoughts which sprang up beside them or which they brought into being; from which came my recommendation to read Hegel in his *Anmerkungen,* or marginal observations, rather than in the paragraphs of his *Encyclopaedia,* directed toward constructing the cathedral of the innumerable triads, enchained one with the other and often with dazzling virtuosity. To single out in him and other thinkers the pure and critical Philosophy of the Spirit, which was in them, from the metaphysics of more or less near theological provenance which framed them or mixed itself up in them, has been my constant care; and in every philosophical work of mine whatsoever I have attempted to give Philosophy of the Spirit, not metaphysics: as in the concreteness of philosophy, which is history, I have wished to give history, pure history, in its only thinkable form, and not an arbitrary metaphysical construction or "Philosophy of History."

Thus, and in this respect also following the example of the men of the Risorgimento, in the loving study of German poetry and literature I detached myself, as was obvious, from the anti-romantic and anti-German men of letters in Italy,[1] but I did not for that reason fall into the admiration for secondary and mediocre poets against which that excellent familiar of German literature, Imbriani,[2] was already protesting in Naples—Imbriani who spared neither Schiller nor Hebbel nor others of their ilk, highflown indeed but geniuses of doubtful alloy. In reality, I recognized in the German language but one very great poet, Wolfgang von Goethe, neither equaled nor approached by any among all the others of his tongue, whose works, almost analogously to what I was doing for the philosophers, I dissolved out from the frequently artificial structures and from the second meanings upon which he was accustomed to support them, and from all the intellectualisms and allegorisms and biographisms with which, in spite of his anticipatory protests, the critics of his country liked to load them down. When my book on Goethe came out, Hermann Bahr expressed his wonder and joy that the method of Italian criticism should have come to remind his fellow-countrymen of the simple truth that Goethe was a creator of poetry and made works of beauty, and thus, and only thus, was to be judged and loved. The historic picture of Italian literature, which nevertheless had been formed with much more rigorous selection than that which befell the literary historiography of other countries, was able to present in the foreground, from the fourteenth to the sixteenth centuries, the "four poets," [3] as they were called by spontaneous

---

[1] For indications on some of these, see my *Letteratura della nuova Italia*, IV, 274-93; VI, 234.

[2] On Imbriani's criticism of German literature see my book on *Goethe* (3rd ed., Bari, 1939), pp. 423-42. (B.C.)

[3] Dante, Petrarch, Ariosto, Tasso. (Tr.)

general agreement, four consummate poetical geniuses. It is true that the German critics and historians of the eighteenth century, at a time when Italy's heart gave forth a Foscolo, a Leopardi and a Manzoni, devoted themselves to belittling Italian poetry, considering it rhetorical, suited only to the light and jocose, and inferior to German poetry, which, it seemed, innately possessed profundity of thought, purity of feeling and spontaneity of form; but precisely this prejudice, which I called "romantic," was taken under examination by me forty years ago and demonstrated to be false,[1] in spite of the fact that it had misled some Italian critics.

This prejudice, what is more, was linked with the theory of race, which found propitious soil in diseased moral romanticism, even though it had not yet arrived at the naturalistic and materialistic fullness to which it has now come under our eyes. It was, at that time, rather a theory of the youth and age of peoples, in which the Latins were assigned the role of the senes effeti, weary and exhausted after having produced the greatness of Rome and fulfilled the ancient world, and the Germans were given the role of youth which had overcome Romanity, created the Middle Ages of chivalry and the crusades, created the modern world by means of the Protestant Reformation, and, after two thousand years, was younger than ever before—not disposed, one might say, to grow up at any time.

With theories like that of race, and of the youth and age of peoples, it is not possible to understand so much as one single page of history; but, although these did not merit serious criticism, several times when the opportunity offered

---

[1] In *Problemi di Estetica* (3rd ed., Bari, 1940), pp. 446-54.

I made them known, now expounding the history of Italian poetry according to Herr Ruth, who attributed what little worth he found in it to the Verjüngung, the rejuvenation, brought to it by German blood, an injection.which however did not give natural and genuine youth, except in Dante, who was excluded from Italian poetry as being too great for it;[1] now tracing the profile of an Italian Germanomaniac whose head had been turned by such doctrines and whose soul had been infused with sadness and desperate pessimism;[2] or again reporting with amusement[3] the discoveries of Houston Chamberlain and Woltmann—and so on in like vein. Furthermore, against the picture Manzoni traces of the Lombards, who (according to him) reduced the whole Italian people to impotence for centuries, I set up the different theory and truth of a German scholar who found himself obliged to state that the Italians had never been spiritually and socially so victorious as they were then, since in a brief space of time they gave the Lombards their language, their literature and their customs, dissolving the northerners without residuum into their own nationality.[4] Nor did I fail, in aesthetics and the criticism of art, to put up an implacable fight against the ill-starred duality of classical art and romantic art, of the art of beauty and the art of passion, of harmonic art and titanic art, which carried in their train all the like divisions which today blight the judgment of art, introducing a schism in the single kingdom of beauty, which the Greeks,

---

[1] *Conversazioni critiche*, III, pp. 259-64.

[2] *La letteratura della nuova Italia*, III, pp. 359-70.

[3] For example, in *Conversazioni critiche*, I, pp. 171-2; *Pegine sparse* (Napoli, 1943), I, pp. 305-6.

[4] *Aneddoti di varia letteratura* (Napoli, 1942), III, pp. 138-9.

Romans, Italians, French and English knew single and alone, and alone reverenced as the criterion of aesthetic reason.

On these three points, then, it does not seem to me that I have gone astray up to now, nor should I excuse myself for any error. But what concept had I formed then of Germany in its political, social and moral aspect? Since I have called this writing "confessions," I shall confess by saying that, in my childhood, I had read many stories and novels of German life, and above all had taken delight in those of the good Canon Schmidt, translated into Italian and printed in Naples in the Bourbon period by Pelagio Rossi, which my mother before me had read and had put into my hands. From these my fancy had been filled with villages whitened by snow and of hospitable little houses in which shone the flame of the household fireplace; of brown castles, of bold and noble knights, lovely and most virtuous maidens, generous actions and high proofs of austere duty, of simple, friendly traits and all the rest of it. This, for me, was Germany; and I believe that because of this childish idyllic dream, so impressed on my mind, the first journey I wanted to make outside of Italy was to Germany, as if to welcome into my soul so much virtue and humankindness from a still living Middle Age. From this journey, in that respect, I returned in some disillusionment, because the many restored castles I saw up there, and the many examples of nineteenth-century false Gothic, cooled me off considerably—besides which I found myself everywhere faced by the pride of the recent triumph over France and with it the ambition to emulate her, as it were the dancing bear, in *grosstädisches Leben*. I marveled too at the adjectivization, to be read frequently in inscriptions, of *Deutsche Treue, Deutsche Tapferkeit*,

Deutsche Grossmut, and I told myself, smiling, that apparently the Germans had confiscated for themselves all the common human virtues.

But, to leave my sentimental vicissitudes, Germany was then esteemed and revered, by me as by my masters and by all Italians, for military power, doctrine, technical capacity and for seriousness in the understanding of life; and the wish was general that Italy in all these respects might rise to be like her; Italians were on the reserve and defensive toward the opposite example of France, thought to be less useful than the much less kindred example which, because less akin, was more strongly educative, as an integration of all that was lacking in Italy.

There is no wonder, then, that after the outbreak of war in 1914 and Italy's entrance into it in 1915, although as a disciplined citizen I had given my vote to the declaration of war and had participated in its fortunes with all my soul, always tense with anxiety and the desire for Italian victory, I did not tolerate, and considered it my duty not to tolerate but to reject the lies, calumnies and insults which then were poured out against Germany, its morality, its culture, its poetry, its science, its philosophy, and of which in Italy I saw the principal propagators to be those same academicians and professors who formerly had been Germany's prostrate admirers and who had not even known how to adopt toward German works that discernment which I for my part had exercised. The war that was being fought was for me, at that time, a political war in the relations of power, hegemony and colonial expansion; not without reason I doubted the ideal motives of liberty and democracy with which it was sought, particularly on the part of the Entente, to beflag it.

Certainly that which followed when the war was won cannot be said to have proved my doubts unfounded. To me it seemed, and insistently and vigorously I said it, that the belligerents ought not to trample upon historic truth as they were doing, ought not to soil works of art and thought, vilifying heroes and men of genius, whether they were German or not, but should attend solely to the business of employing their arms without ruining ours, that is to say, those arms which are the common force of all humanity, a patrimony jealously to be preserved intact. Such was my argument during the war, to which practical work was added with perfect coherency after the establishment of peace, when, both as a private citizen and as a minister in the Giolitti cabinet, I exerted myself to facilitate the return of Germans to Italy, to bring about the restitution of their property and the restitution to the German state or to their proprietors of the scientific institutions they had founded in Italy—upon which the hands of the Italian academicians and professors had already been laid—and so on, endeavoring on my part to restore esteem and concord between the Italians and Germans, whom I saw at that time reappearing among us, timid and obsequious, and into whom I was sometimes obliged to infuse a little pride by reminding them of the great gestures and great ordeals of Germany up to and including the lost war. Arms had decided as they had decided; the diplomats and politicians had put together a rickety peace, which quivered and quaked in every part; but I hoped that reciprocal acquaintance, and the resumption of investigations and of meditations and of the exchanges of thought, might mature a better Europe and inspire a wiser policy.

Germany itself seemed, with the Weimar Republic, to be directed toward that political life of liberty which she had never deeply felt and had only feebly possessed and practiced during the preceding seventy years but which—who knows?—young as she was at least in this respect (the Germans who visited me in Rome at the time of my ministry said to me sometimes that they had come to learn liberal practices in Italy: in Italy which was even then unconsciously preparing for Fascism!), she might have instilled with a fervor born of the very misfortunes she owed to nationalism, militarism and imperial authoritarianism, and together with that the intense and disciplined industriousness which was her virtue compared to all other peoples. Almost with hesitation, as one who feels the red rising to his face for the lost liberty of his own fatherland, I made up my mind to go to Germany for an academic ceremony in 1927, when, in spite of the troubles of the political parties which prevented strong or durable governments, the country had picked itself up economically and seemed rich and hardworking (or even joyous and exuberant, as in an orgy of naked flesh by Rubens), and the clear words of Stresemann inspired confidence at home and abroad. But already, some years previously, the welcome given the advent of Fascism in Italy by the newborn democratic and liberal Germany made me thoughtful: I used to receive regularly, at that time, the *Preussische Jahrbücher*, and I have in my mind a phrase which I read there with stupor and bitter disgust, which said more or less as follows: that the Germans cared nothing whatever about the anguished hearts of the Italian liberals, but that they saluted in the chief of Fascism a "disturber (*Verstörer*) of the European peace."

Received with much cordiality wherever I went, and honored with degrees and diplomas by their universities and academies, I heard from more than one person that, in spite of the great esteem they cherished for me, they were obliged to declare that they admired our great man, Signor Mussolini (who was getting ready, from a distance, for the moment when he was to be christened by Hitler "the greatest man generated by Italy since the fall of the Roman Empire").

A lady of the diplomatic world, who had been my good friend ever since she lived in Naples in her youth, repeated the same admiration to me, and when I asked why, she replied: "I admire him as I admire you, because he is, like you, a surging fountain of vitality, a truly Italian spectacle."

A Protestant pastor and philosophical writer, who was the best editor and commentator on the published and unpublished works of Hegel, having invited me to his house, also expressed his admiration for the same personage.

"Why?"

"Because," he pronounced solemnly, "he has put into effect the great Hegelian idea of the corporate state."

"First of all, this was not one of Hegel's great ideas, but merely a badly thought-out combination of Prussian reactionary inspirations; and furthermore that person has put it into effect *auf Papier*, on paper only."

And so it went.

A friend who had been pleased by an essay of mine just then published, *The Conflicts of Political Ideals after 1870*, wanted to translate and publish it in one of the principal newspapers of Berlin; but, after various attempts, he wrote me that he was obliged to renounce the idea, because some of my words of faith in the liberal development of Germany had provoked the reply: "that the author, esteemed though he was, had understood nothing that was stirring the heart of Germany." What was stirring it was, in fact, Nazism: which truly I had not understood.

Nor was it easy to understand; so far from it that when I returned there in October, 1931, and found the country very different from what it had been four years earlier, as a result of the grave industrial crisis, the daily and growing clashes between Nazis and Communists and the extremely difficult position of the successive governments, I still did not hear anywhere an expectation, or even a timorous suspicion, of the triumph of Hitler. I remember a political conference in which a churchman politely and intelligently answered the representatives of the various parties, but when he came to those of the Nazis: "To you," he said, "I have nothing to say, because you are simply insane."

At Frankfort, in the house of a lady, among political and literary men who had been invited to meet me, discussing the political factions which were fighting each other in the country, I asked one of them, Simon, the director of the *Frankfurter Zeitung,* what he thought was going to happen, and he replied: "I am convinced that nothing will happen. The German people is very intelligent."

However, a little more than a year later, he had lost his newspaper and had been constrained to take refuge in France.

The same disposition, anything but pessimistic, I noted in other and remarkable men with whom I talked at the time, such as Einstein and Thomas Mann, firm liberals who greatly deplored Fascism in Italy, but who did not (it seems to me) even suspect the much greater ruin which was drawing near for Germany, and who perhaps became aware of it only when they too were forced into exile.

However, when Hitler and his own had truly come into dominion over Germany and announced their dominion by the violent persecution of the Jews, by the burning of books by unacceptable writers, and by the absolute racist theory, biological and naturalistic as it had never been up to that moment, I, in harmony with the defense I had formerly made of Germany during the 1914-1918 war against the calumnies used against her by writers of the Entente, undertook, in the cultural and political notes of the review *La Critica*, the defense of science, culture, morality and good sense against Nazi Germany: a polemic in which, at a given point, I desisted, because there was no longer any object in pursuing it.

"When it sprinkles," we say in such cases, "open the umbrella; but when it pours rain, get into the doorway and close the umbrella."

Even so, I took the occasion of a request made to me in August, 1936, by the *Nation* of Berne to comment upon the recent substitution, ordered by the Nazis, of the inscription on the front of the University of Heidelberg: *To the Living Spirit*, by the other *To the German Spirit*, to discourse upon "The Germany We Loved," in an article translated into German and also published in Italian in *La Critica*. On account of this article, an able German papyrologist and Greek scholar, who had frequented my house in Naples years before when he was studying the papyri of Herculaneum here, and who had been concerned solely with those fragments which for that matter he did not

succeed in reading or integrating, and who, in the new turn
taken by his country, had set aside his Greek and become an
ardent Nazi, devoting himself to the work of fabricating,
as I was told, according to Hitler's ideas, the "German Man"
(upon which I may allow my sarcasms to go unsaid) addressed an open letter to me, printed in pamphlet form at
Lorrach in 1937, under the title: *An den Deutschen-Freund
B.C. in Neapel, damit er uns besser verstehe: über Deutsch-
land gegenwartigen Erneuerung und Zukunft des Deutschen
Geistes* ("To the friend-of-the-Germans B.C. in Naples, so
that he may understand us better: on the present renewal of
Germany and on the future of the German spirit"). But I
had then understood them so well that for this very reason
I had given my farewell to "the Germany I had loved." I
had remained the same always; Germany had not.

And even on the new conditions of Germany I finished
by remaining silent because I was already combating them
implicitly by my opposition to our own Fascism, which,
after having in the voice of its chief insulted the German
people, up to and including its physical aspect, in the most
vulgar and trivial manner, after having endeavored to set
alight a European war in order to suffocate Nazi Germany
at the outset, after having protected the persecuted Jews
from Germany and accepted homage from them (which they
should have abstained from presenting if in them, over
miserable private and contingent interests, there had prevailed the other feeling that Nazism and Fascism had a common root in the negation of human liberty), after having
gone so far as to move Italian troops on to the Brenner
Pass as a threat against the first attempt at occupation of
Austria—after all this—finished by joining Nazism in a sense-

less and pernicious alliance, of which, and of the fruits which it matured and which we in the opposition painfully foresaw, there is no use in speaking again, because they are in plain view of all. Among our many misfortunes was this: the chief of Fascism happened to come from the elementary schoolteacher's level of cultural preparation and therefore had not even learned a bit of that Latin which is taught in the first classes of secondary school; he had not present in his mind, as we all have, the admonitory fable of Phaedrus on how dangerous it may be *cum potente societas*.[1]

There was, for that matter, a deep and intimate difference between Nazism and Fascism, because the first was a terrible crisis which had been brooding in the history of Germany through centuries, and the second was a superfetation foreign to the history of Italy through the centuries and repugnant to the recent and glorious Italian history of the nineteenth century; the first had both a tragic and a diabolical aspect, and the second, even in the midst of the crimes it committed, in the midst of the destruction and the ruins, kept an invincibly clownlike aspect, as anybody could see at first glance by contrasting the appearances of the two chiefs. I had tried to explain this pedagogically to the Nazi Greek scholar one evening, among other things telling him, who had been talking of the new community of ideas between Italy and Germany, that, all things considered, "We Italians were greatly superior to the Germans."

---

[1] Croce refers to Aesop's fable of the sheep who made friends with his powerful neighbor the wolf. The fables are known to every Italian secondary-school boy through the simple metrical versions of Phaedrus, a Latin writer of the fourth century. (Tr.)

"Superior, why?" he asked me with that attentive air of the German who is always trying to listen and learn.

"Because," I answered, "our Italians, which is to say those of us who play the Fascist, know that they are acting in complete bad faith, but you Germans believe in it for true."

"And what is the superiority in that?"

"This: that we, with our bad faith, at least keep the intellect lucid, and we remain bad men, but men: whereas you lose it altogether and become beasts."

On this point, Nazism considered as a very grave crisis because it is one result of the whole history of a people, I meditated and made researches, in order to become thoroughly aware of it, in all its maze; and I proposed to write about this in due course—some things I did indeed write in some pages which have remained unpublished. But the conclusions I reached, which gave me the clarity of intelligence necessary for the correlative attitudes and for political and moral resolutions, were anticipated in the meanwhile, written out in a most exact formula, and convalidated, by a letter sent me from a learned German who had lived a long time in Italy and whose name, since he is absent, I shall keep to myself. I transcribe his words here, because they are words of truth, nourished by long studies of the subject, and because it is appropriate to publish them today and offer them to the meditation of all, of all men on all sides, so high is the thought and so great is the patriotic grief and desire for good expressed therein. It is well not to forget that in Germany there are still men and intellects that feel and think like this.

"Of the war years," he says, "I do not wish to speak. When the monstrous attack on the world's liberty was re-

vealed, I was so stricken that for four years I refused to read
the newspaper or listen to the radio, asking my familiars
not to mention to me the news of what was happening daily
in Poland, Belgium and Russia, because I needed to take
shelter in order not to destroy in my own conscience the
thought which for fifty-five years had led me through the
crimes of history, those crimes which constantly threaten
to root out all love of one's country. This thought is simple,
as my own conduct has been single-voiced and transparent,
as if the rays of a clear internal light passed through the
delicate surface of a physiognomy which was not that of a
pachyderm. I love my country, and because I love it I respect
every other country; the man to whom all mothers are not
sacred cannot know the *pietas* he owes to his own mother.
I knew that the war must be lost, and that whoever wished
for victory was blind, because thus he was wishing upon
Europe centuries of wars of extermination. I knew that my
fatherland did not have and could not have the qualities
necessary for governing peoples and freeing the slave; indeed, the indomitable fury of delusion and the fixed idea
of a faith not kept wheel round in its abstract brain like the
tiger caught in a trap, and consume it as fire consumes
straw; precisely these excesses demonstrate that it cannot
govern yet, but must indeed be governed. In many respects,
it is the most able people in Europe, as in other respects it is
gifted with profound genius; but nature and history have
betrayed it, attaching to it three almost organic deficiencies
of which it is not conscious, but which indeed it cultivates
as if they were its best virtues.

"In its cerebral structure metaphysical thought prevails
so greatly, and with such force of suggestion, that it works

almost with the primordial energy of passion; this inevitably leads to criminal fanaticism if it is not anchored in the depths of nature.

"History has furthermore done the German people the grave wrong of sparing it up to the present time the experience of a long and hard serfdom under the heel of the foreigner—an experience from which are born the idea of liberty and the sense of need for it, as happened in Ireland, Poland, Italy and Saxon England. This is a spiritual deficit with the gravest consequences, which history could perhaps cure only by the application of heroic means.

"The third deficiency, the most desperate of all, was the result of the battle between Arminius and Varus in 9 B.C.: of that battle which decided the Romans to renounce forever the Romanization of Germany, abandoning that country to itself. Between all the other European regions there evidently exists a delicate and not very easy to grasp, but powerfully efficacious, activity of the internal form of the spirit, as also of the mode of conceiving, on certain heights, the relations of thought and feeling, which affinities, like the dome of the ether, are raised in unity above their national differences, thus constituting a sphere in the limpidity of which are harmlessly dissolved those earthly exhalations which, if they could not reach such heights, would finish by producing sharp material conflicts. This affinity emanates from the inexhaustible vitality of Latin culture, common for centuries to all the clans from which modern nations have developed; while the Germans, as an effect of the aforesaid battle, remained excluded from that commonalty, which they, in spite of the Renaissance and all their studies of classical philology, have never succeeded in re-establishing because they lost their contact with it too early. This is also the source from which pour the eternal complaints of the Germans that they are not understood or that they are maliciously interpreted, plaints that often are in bad faith, but create that latent irritation which more than seldom, being provoked by casual incidents, breaks out in violent reactions. With these and other thoughts, which are known to some of my friends, I have been able to find a way out of the labyrinth of my conscience and to impose a peace upon the opposition of conflicting feelings; and the need to act in this way was so much the more urgent in proportion as the abyss between the two nations began to open out deeper and deeper."

Furthermore, he adds:

"I hope that when Germany is judged, the Anglo-Saxons will avoid the errors of the Treaty of Versailles and of its execution. Let them take away from Germany even the left bank of the Rhine, but let them spare her the poisonous humiliations, those deep cancerous wounds of the soul which make men savage, drive them mad, and prevent one man from enclosing himself with his own conscience. Further, in judging the German people let it not be forgotten that it —that Treaty also has no little responsibility in the degeneration of the German soldier, which made easy for Hitler his impious speculation on the weakness of the German brain."

That which, with such wisdom, is deduced and reasoned from history in the pages of this letter, is what I have defined as "the spiritual dissension between Germany and Europe": a dissension, a discord, which historians must investigate and make known in all its preparation from afar back, when it slithered in the subsoil of German life; in any case, only this dissension offered a full explanation of certain actions and certain events in German and European history up to our days, in which we have seen it break out and stand before us in all its fury of offense and defense. Offense and defense in the mad but nevertheless terrible form of an attack against Europe and against the whole world on the part of a people which, calling itself a race and an elect race, wishes to conduct all the others *not* to a higher civilization by means of higher ideas—as Greece and Rome and Italy and France and England did in certain periods of their history—but wishes to enslave them all to its power without ideas, *nominor quia leo* or some other even less noble beast.

But from this historic delineation, which will be the most urgent and living problem of the historian in the immediate future and which is clearly, although summarily traced out in this little work, it is time to pass on to that which is and will be the most urgent moral and political problem of our own time, in which must travail not only the present but further generations of men. We pass on to it only in order to put down, as best one can, some directing concepts which perhaps are different from and opposed to those which many have in mind and which would conduct them only into erroneous courses, vain works and pernicious results.

Because in the first place, that which comes out of what we have said here, and which must be put forward as a premise, is that the evil to be cured has an historical nature, was historically born and will historically die; therefore it does not possess the character of a fantastic fact in physics, or rather in metaphysics, conferred upon it by the concept of race, the unreal and transcendental essence of which, in its turbid oriental religiosity, was clearly seen by Tocqueville when he saw it spread out before him in the books of his friend Gobineau. What a misfortune it would be if race were that which the Nazis and the philosophers of Nazism believe! The Germans in that case would be outside of history and of humanity, irreducible to the former and unredeemable for the latter. But this concept is a phantasm of disordered and incoherent imaginations—as are, by reaction, the excogitations which nowadays are springing up in flighty brains, of murders to be carried out in mass in order to diminish the number of Germans, of sterilizations on the example given by the Nazis themselves, or of chopping up Germany into little states to which all union or federation would be forbidden, supposing them for this reason easier to watch over. Multiple foolishness thus replies to folly, thinking so to defeat it. But foolishness can be dissolved only by reasonableness, which alone is capable likewise of resisting the blind impulses of passion, even when those were originally set in motion by moral indignation.

In the second place, since the dissension between Germany and Europe which history has called forth can and must be composed by history, it is quite clear that toward this end all the forces of European civilization should tend, with all means that present themselves when and as they become necessary, from rigor to indulgence, from exclusion to collaboration, from severity to cordiality, from conflict to conciliation; upon this there is no longer any need to dwell, all the more because not a few, in England and in America, have understood this necessity and have begun to meditate around it, expounding concepts and designs which are both human and wise. But the action of others, as is also clear, can never resolve a problem of mind and heart in the individual or in the single people and must be resolved by that individual or single people. The failure of this gigantic major attempt to effect with force and violence the dream of dominion over Europe, and, by means of Europe, over the world, this failure, which follows so many others in German history, beginning with the Roman Empire of the German Nation with Italy united to it as "the garden of the Empire," and follows at a little distance of years a preceding world war, should be the last experiment which will produce in the German people the necessary catharsis and induce it to take its place in humanity, not as the barbaric master and butcher, but as one of the peoples among peoples, one of the strongest among them in the struggle which is intrinsic to the life of humanity and civilization. And the shame which it cannot help but feel over the evil for which it has made itself the instrument will be converted into a force of good—as with those great saints who were once great sinners.

To these pages of my confessions are added the article mentioned as of 1936: *The Germany We Loved*, as well as two other brief essays which form part of my *Various Philosophical Discourses* and were composed as clarifications, the first on a point of historiographical methodology and the other on a point of the science of ethics, but which, by the exemplification of which they make use, have direct reference to the ideology and psychology of the Germans; and, at the end, an epigraph which it befell me to dictate at the request of a generous American journalist, recalling one of the innumerable acts of inhuman ferocity accomplished during these months in a short strip of the territory of

Southern Italy by German soldiers, who every day are increasing the quantity and ferocity of such acts. How many horrifying stories are reaching me now of the burned, sacked, bloodied and outraged places of my native Abruzzo! However, even in this epigraph there is not lacking the word which historically circumscribes the evil, calling the German "the present enemy of humanity": present and not future, contingent and not eternal, as Nazism would have wished it to be for the eternal terror and trembling of the world.

Sorrento, December 28, 1943

The Germany we loved

The Germany we loved[1]

DURING the war we were told by Germany's adversaries that German philosophy, science and poetry were manifestations of the same barbaric spirit and an instrument of the same policy of overbearing arrogance against which civil humanity was defending itself with arms, and that it was therefore correct to drive them out of our souls and from our schools. Today from many Germans, or rather from a choral voice which in contemporary Germany silences all the others, we are told that in fact it does not matter what the other peoples feel or think of German philosophy, science and poetry, because these are things purely their own and peculiar to their people, expressions of the individuality of the race, and therefore the other peoples can never either feel them or understand them.

To the adversaries in wartime we answered, then, that poetry, philosophy and science are neither German nor of any particular people, but belong to pure humanity; and, against their injunctions, we continued to prize and to study those works written in the German language. To the present Germanomaniacs and racists one is constrained (weird irony

---

[1] Written for *Die Nation* of Berne; published in German in April, 1936, and in Italian at the same time in *La Critica*.

of things!) to repeat exactly the same things that one said to their extreme opponents, adding (even if this should wound them and make them furious) the tranquil declaration that those works are ours no less than theirs, because they belong to everybody who can understand and love them; and perhaps today they are more ours than theirs, because the Germans do not respect them in their truth, but distort them to their special ends, deliberately misunderstanding or falsifying them.

It is not possible to expound briefly the complicated historic process in which national pride and boasting, which from time to time are seen to flame out in all peoples, came to take in Germany the form of a scientific doctrine, with such effect that the nationalisms of the other peoples, in the nineteenth century, attempted to imitate it, even though in such a way that, as is usual in imitations, they showed themselves less sure of themselves and more fragile. One might trace a prehistory of racism which would go back to the barbarian invasions and would have its solemn monument in the famous reply of Liutprando, bishop of Cremona, to the Byzantine emperor: that "we Lombards, and with us the Saxons, Franks, Lotharingians, Swabians and Burgundians, understand by Roman *quicquid ignobilitatis, quicquid timiditatis, quicquid avaritiae, quicquid luxuriae, quicquid mendacii, immo quicquid vitiorum est*, characteristics very worthy of a people issued from a collection of turpitudinous clans and baptized in the blood of the fratricide of Romulus" (*De legat. constantin.*, 12); and, following on down, one could pursue the continuous tradition through the Middle Ages and afterwards in the age of the Renaissance and the Reformation. But the true history of the elevation of that feeling to a scientific doctrine has its mental origins in the persistence with which in Germany, longer than anywhere else, there were preserved, along with the Biblical idea of a chosen people and the Augustinian idea of predestination, the schema of the succession of empires: all things which afterwards, during the nineteenth century, were laicized, covering themselves with a philosophical garment, as can be seen in a terminal and in every respect classical work, Hegel's *Philosophy of History*. The rising of the nationalities against the Napoleonic domination, which was not directly founded upon this doctrine, but upon the pressing need of independence and liberty, favored it at all events in a certain measure, taking from it sometimes, for other uses, rhetorical colors and arguments. Thus was introduced into the vision of a single human history the schism of the "Germanic" and the "non-Germanic," which shattered in two also the sphere of poetry and art, thanks to the calamitous divisions of ingenuous and sentimental art, classical and romantic, Latin and Germanic, or, in more modern formulae, of the art "of beauty" and "titanic art," of "closed form" and "open form," and the like, from which today's German criticism of art remains habitually a prisoner and suffers not a little. When the religious sense was lost, and also the philosophical and categorical sense (that of characteristics and missions assigned to the various peoples), materialism prevailed, and the same distinctions and divisions were materialized by the zoological concept of race, of superior race and inferior race, one strong and the other weak, one destined to command and the other to serve. Tocqueville pointed out at once to his friend Gobineau—not a German, but one of the principal authors of this transformation, with a great following in Germany—that in his physiologism and materialism there was fermenting a great deal of Augustinianism, Calvinism and Jansenism, dominated by a substantial pessimism about humanity. At all events, up until a few years ago these doctrines, even though they had no small success, encountered in Germany itself critical intellects which held them in doubt or practically ignored them, abandoning them almost altogether to the writers of sensational books, composed for the great public which delights in dazzling discoveries and simplicist explanations, like those of Houston Chamberlain and others of the ilk. The grave thing that has occurred in recent years is that these doctrines have become official and institutional and inform corresponding political actions and practical provisions in the schools as in propaganda and popular education.

Certainly the natural and historical conditions of a people offer material to its thought and to its art; but even so the material, however necessary it may be, is material and is not form, with which it cannot coincide and by which it cannot be causally determined but which must burn the material in its fire and obtain from it its light, or, as Schiller said, "destroy" it (vertilgt). Nor, on the other hand, do thinkers and poets have as their only material the needs and sentiments of their own people, whether because these needs and sentiments themselves vibrate in the life of the vast world to which they are linked, or because thinkers and poets breathe always in the vast world, in the universe, without which they could not fulfill their work, even the most modest work. In fact, when anybody conceives the strange proposition of making thinkers and poets express the sentiments and needs of a given people or of a given state regime, it is necessary to

have recourse to authority and force, and to command determined scientific conclusions and determined artistic con-
figurations: with the inevitable results that the things thus
produced are neither science nor art, but, in conformity with
their genesis, are practical and political acts, for which the
man of taste and the lover of truth will have no use and
which, even as practical political acts, will turn out sterile
and superfluous, since, in all truth, the aid which the states-
man can obtain from bad verses and foolish elucubrations is
not great. Frederick II of Prussia, who was an absolute king
but also a man of acute intelligence, said it was necessary
to allow liberty to the scientific and literary press, as otherwise "it would not be interesting." The dilemma is in-
exorable: either the works of thought and poetry avail themselves of all material and rise above all material in the
ideality of form; or else they remain more or less bogged
down into the material, whether it is political or even merely
of individual or private interest, and in that case they cease
to be works of poetry or thought in proportion to their en-
tanglement. The criticism of art and the criticism of philosophy continually discern those works, and those parts
of works, which are practical intentions simulating thought
and poetry; that is to say, they discern the true from the false
and the beautiful from the ugly. Even in a powerful philosophical mind like that of Hegel are to be seen pseudo-
philosophical elements, which led him—it seems incredible—
to conclude the drama of the world's history with the
Prussian State of the Restoration.

Therefore it is impossible to develop, as they say they
wish and are attempting to do, the history of thought and
poetry as they flowered in Germany, in the guise of a closed

history, formed by means of distinctly German forces in the origins and in the development, past, present and future. It would be too easy to disprove this sort of historiography, so far as antiquity and the Middle Ages are concerned, by recalling the work of Rome and of the Latin pontificate, without adding that the primitive German age itself, before the barbarian invasions, was anything but enclosed within itself. Modern philology comes to demonstrate that in medieval literature, where it was once believed that we faced an autochthonous popular poetry, there is always to be found the efficacy of the Roman writers as model. It is too easy to recall what German humanism owed to Italian humanism and the Reformation itself to European mysticism and to the medieval heresies against the Church of Rome; and how Italian, Spanish and French literature worked upon German letters in the seventeenth and eighteenth centuries; and how and to what degree the personality of a Leibnitz was European. But, even if we consider only the great German epoch, celebrated for its originality, that which was the first and true affirmation of Germany in the domain of culture, that which is her most refulgent glory, even this shows itself not as an infusion of "Germanism" (and nobody knows what that might be!) in the life of Europe and the world, but as an enforcement and fulfillment of that same European and world life. At that time—it is said and it is well said— German thought laid the foundations of the religion of the modern age, intending to render the transcendent immanent, profane history sacred, and putting into labor, which continuously amplifies and enlarges life, the human ideal; it gave the objective and dialectical sense of history, rejected intellectualistic and rationalistic abstractions, restored, as against illuministic illusions, a more severe concept of politics and of the state, claimed the autonomy and dignity of fancy and of poetry, explored the methods of modern linguistics and philology; and so onward. And nevertheless each one of these works of thought had behind it not emptiness but fullness, the preceding work of European thought; not only the intellectual positions which these works had to deny and surpass but which even so were necessary steps, but also the links to which they positively attached themselves. Whoever investigates the history of ideas is led to this recognition; and, to point out only recent studies, it is already known that the ideas on the State and on politics, counterposed to illuminism in Germany, come from the study of Macchiavelli and of the Italian tractarians on the *raison d'état*; that Baumgarten's *Aesthetics* was anticipated by Vico and the Italian tractarians on poetics, from whom on another side Lessing descends, as Winckelmann does from Bellori and other Italian critics of art; and that Kant's *Critique of Pure Reason* found its elements above all in the English theorists on taste and on genius; that the polemic against Jacobinism in the name of history and of tradition was made, before the Germans did it, by the Englishman Burke and the Frenchman De Maistre; that the cult of the Gothic and other romantic predilections of that order came from England; that methodology in the editing of texts and the historical criticism of evidence had been carried very far forward in Italy by Muratori; that Shaftesbury and Rousseau, Voltaire and Montesquieu, Robertson and Gibbon were masters for the German moralists and historians; that Goethe is no less European than Leibnitz, Goethe whose very literary form presupposes the long refinement which the baroque and the rococo, on the Italian and French model, brought about in German language, culture and style; not to say that without Hume there could be no Kant, and without Bruno, Descartes and Spinoza, neither Schelling nor Hegel. In so saying we do not dispute the originality of the great German poet and the great thinkers; but, simply, we reject the child-ish idea of originality as a function of a people or of a race. Their originality was their personality itself and their genius. For the rest, the greatest of these philosophers, writers and poets felt themselves to be cosmopolites, and even (conforming thus to Lutheran directives) maintained a certain in-difference toward politics, practical struggles and the so-called national interests, considering that they paid their whole debt in this regard by homage and obedience to the prince. Goethe never betrayed too much tenderness for whatever was "German" in art. If an occasional nationalistic attitude was assumed among some of them, as an effect of the wars against Napoleon or for other similar motives, it remained secondary and did not corrupt their higher work.

Thus is explained the fact that the new German thought and poetry, in the intellectual exuberance which followed the wars of the Revolution and Empire, were welcomed in the whole of Europe, most of all in France, and its books were studied, translated, commented upon and imitated. Europe was prepared for them: in those books it found solutions of problems which had beset and were still be-setting it, elaborations of concepts which had been sketched out before, conclusions and systematizations to which Europe had already approached or toward which it was proceeding. There was to be found even the necessary as-sistance for the correction and integration of its rationalistic concept of liberty in the historic concept of liberalism: a crisis of great importance, taking place notably in France during the Restoration, upon which I have insisted on other occasions, wondering that the German writers have not made more of it and have not derived satisfaction from the efficacy thus exercised by their historical philosophy on the maturing of the liberal ideal and, thereby, upon all the noblest history of the nineteenth century. Now, if these works had been "the quintessence of Germanism," they would have remained foreign to European culture; but, in effect, in turning to Kant, Fichte, Goethe and Hegel, that culture turned toward its own sons, who had fulfilled and followed out that which other sons had prepared and foreseen, but up to then had not attained.

By the wealth and importance of its intellectual work, Germany assumed, in the imaginations of seekers after truth, of the students and the learned of the nineteenth century, the form which Italy and Rome had had and still had for the Germans: a country of ideal and also effective pilgrimage, since many then visited it and went to its universities. The author of this essay, as a young man, frequented Italian personages—of those we call "men of the Risorgimento" because they worked for the independence, liberty and unity of Italy—and from their teaching absorbed this idea of Germany as fountainhead and guide of modern thought, not without receiving at the same time a certain pious credulity and superstition to the effect that what the Germans continued to write still had a seriousness and a profundity not to be found in the books of other languages.

That was a most resplendent epoch, but so little was it a function of a certain people or race that it passed; it passed like the Hellas of Pericles, the Italy of the Renaissance, the France of Louis XIV: human history makes efforts like these, in which a flowering of men of genius comes to the world, only at intervals of centuries or millennia. Already around 1830 ardent zealots of German culture in France, such as Quinet and Michelet, gave warning that in the Germany of the day there were, amongst many epigones, few original personalities. Apart from the industry of the German universities which never faltered, German thought descended from the heights to which it had raised itself; it became timid in philosophy, putting itself into the train of the natural sciences, timid in history, which grew to be separate from that philosophy to which it had been welded in the classic age; and in the period of positivism, evolutionism and sociologism German thought did not even occupy the first positions any longer, as these were held by Englishmen, Frenchmen and Italians. And so little (it is well to repeat) was the intellectual and practical power of other days a function of political power and of the race, that, when Germany rose to the united and imperial state, and caused its authority and its power to weigh heavily upon the world, its thought and its poetry no longer gave forth fruits like those of yore. The least inelegant of the philosophies it produced in that era was the so-called "theory of values," substantially a derivation from the old Herbartism. The most famous philosophical writer, Nietzsche, was certainly not remarkable for speculative or logical vigor: he brought no progress to any theory in any field of philosophy, neither in logic nor in ethics nor in aesthetics. He was, more than anything else, an agitated soul and, at times, a splendid writer, a symptom of the restlessness of the times and not a creator of new directive principles. The classical German philosophers still maintained admirers and disciples in England, Italy and even in France (the link between Bergson and Schelling by way of Ravaisson is well known); but in their own country—when they were not forgotten or ignored and were not regarded with disdainful superiority as "metaphysicists" or "fantasists"—they formed the object of scholastic expositions and erudite researches, and even, sometimes, were taken as excuses for the so-called "revivals" which are always wishfulness and impotence. German culture, once universal and cosmopolitan, sympathetic toward those of the other peoples, restricted itself to its own national circle and finished by no longer understanding even its own great men, whose nature demanded that they be displayed against the background of the world and not of one region. And then there took place what has taken place: it can be symbolized by two anecdotes. There is the case of the *Review for the Philosophy of Culture*, which changed its name to *Review for the German Philosophy of Culture*. And there is the other, just recently, of the inscription on the front of the University of Heidelberg, *To the Living Spirit*, now replaced by the different dedication: *To the German Spirit*.

But in our hearts still lives the Germany of thought and poetry, that which we have devotedly loved and still ever love. We love it not only in its great era and in its great authors, but also in everything of theirs that we can still see shining through in so many German men who, under adverse conditions, continue together with us those concepts and those ideals, looking toward the future.

War as ideal

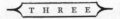

War as ideal

IT can be said that a first and serious, although unexpressed and implicit, assertion of anti-militaristic thought took place in the history of historiography when (in the nineteenth century) boredom and irritation developed toward books entirely made up of accounts of wars and of negotiations preparing or concluding them. There arose the insistent demand for another form of history which would give what truly corresponded to the major interests of the human mind and soul: the history of religion, of philosophy, of science, of the arts, of customs and moral life, and, in a word, the history of civilization. Along this line modern historiography moved, always going forward, not only restricting the too large field which formerly had been given to matters of war, but infusing even in its accounts of these a spirit of which they had been deprived before, referring them to the development of the spiritual life in all its forms, which lowers wars into the status of its instruments and their effects to the material of its ever-new labor. Even the history of warfare as a technique, as one of the various techniques of human endeavor, is an aspect of this spiritual history, and more directly of the history of applied science. But war, considered as war in itself, does not lend itself to any historical in-

67

telligence, since it cannot be referred to a proper category
or ideal of its own.

In fact, this is a fever which periodically flares up in the
veins of men and in the course of which individuals and peoples, whatever may be their qualities or the elevation of their
rank, fight to overcome and to destroy one another. The
vicissitudes of this struggle can be followed, by anyone who
looks upon them detached and from afar or reads of them in
books, with a lively participation of the imagination and a fel-
low-feeling equal to or stronger than those with which one
watches the spectacles of the circus or the wrestling ring or
the cinema; but substantially they are reduced to a mo-
notonous beating and being beaten, in which luck has great
play and which is not reducible to historical configuration,
because the nexus or let us say the logic and the historical
significance are to be found elsewhere.

And, as in historiography, with the development of superior mental interest, with the progress from chronicle to
historicity, the accounts of wars have been overcome and
dissolved in the manner indicated: thus in human societies,
progressively as they removed themselves from savage and
barbaric conditions (like those of the medieval renewal of
barbarism in which battle was daily and general), and,
breathing more deeply, other orders of facts and works called
upon the soul, war faded from the horizon and sometimes
humanity appeared to have outgrown that condition to the
return of which all civilly educated men, lovers of peace and
industry, felt a repugnance as to criminal insanity. Not that
military institutions were any the less attentively and
jealously cared for, since the intimate conscience warns us
that war cannot be suppressed from the world and that it is

necessary to keep them ready in case of need, as we keep doc-
tors and medicines and surgical instruments ready for a
malady that may always begin again. In the years of our Risorgimento, even during the necessary wars, men always looked
forward to that which is above wars, and the longed-for Italy
showed itself (as a verse of Tommaseo says), "severe and
humble, armed and loving." [1] This state of feeling endured
even after 1871, and was disturbed in Italy, as more strongly
in other parts of Europe, only at the end of the century; and
at that time there was written in England, against the
threatening idea of a war which the inexpert courted, a very
wise book called *The Great Illusion*,[2] which received universal praise. And then when, in spite of everything, the new
fever, the new war, which took the name of the European
conflagration, was set alight some years later, and at last
had been dominated and spent, that state of mind of aversion
to war immediately formed itself again in some of the major
peoples of the two worlds. War was feared by them as a
disease, and not exalted as an ideal.

Now, how has it come about that, in spite of this stage
attained in civilization, in spite of this general good sense,
war in some intellectual currents has in fact been made to
conform to an ideal, to a sublime, resplendent and inebriat-
ing ideal? And that for the concept "war-disease" has been
substituted the other of "war-superior-health"? And that the
continual struggle in which we are accustomed to symbolize
life, which is "war against war," a "negation of negation,"
as we say in philosophical terms, a continual re-establish-

---

[1] "Severa e umile, armata e amante." (Tr.)
[2] By Norman Angell, 1910. (Tr.)

ment ever and ever higher of the internal unity and harmony and social collaboration against the forces which always tend to break or to interrupt it, has received in its own content that against which it fights? And that instead of the image of the honest man who takes arms because of duty and not by taste for warmaking, and through duty attains strength, courage and the spirit of sacrifice, imaginations have created or made idols representing others very different —unheard-of beings whose appearance, voices and manners are warlike, rapacious and obsessed by butchery and destruction?

Undoubtedly such a disturbance of the intellect and imagination is to be traced to that retrograde romanticism, strongly sensualist and materialistic, which was called decadence, which ignored and wounded many delicate sentiments, soiled and corrupted many pure affections, contaminating them with libido and sadism. Moreover it corrupted the virile and dutiful resolution to fight in the wars which the world's course might make necessary, transforming it into the criminal folly of exalting and provoking and instigating war, which is equivalent to deliberately engendering the diseases which are to be cured; and at the same time it corrupted noble and humanitarian traditional patriotism into a sort of ferocious bestiality which to begin with took the name of "nationalism."

With all this, such an ideal or counter-ideal would probably have exhausted itself in the realm of inflated and empty literature, if it had not found its point of support in a people at the very center of Europe, which made of it the directive idea of moral and political life, giving up that much or little of universalism and cosmopolitanism which shines forth in

its great philosophical-poetic age, and rendering itself sealed
and deaf to any understanding of the substantial teaching of
Kant or Goethe. It would be a very insufficient and moreover
improper explanation to say that Germany, lately arrived at
unity and the power that unity gave her, had been seized by
the need of expansion and dominion against other peoples
holding world empire. Such a need would have been able to
seek and find satisfaction by means of policy, and even upon
occasion by arms and war, without any necessity for thereby
poisoning the very springs of moral life, as resulted from
the support which decadent romanticism encountered not
even in the political interests but in the ideal traditions of
Germany—which (it is always well to remember) does not
have the civilization of Greece and Rome and that of Christianity at the origins of its national history and participation
in European history, but the ferocity and devastatory impulse
of the barbarian invasions. Its heroes of those days were no
other than the chiefs of hordes, and its epic certainly does
not present the human figures of the epic of Greece and
Rome or even of the French, not Achilles, Hector and
Aeneas, not Roland and Oliver, neither Andromache nor
Lucretia, but those of somber cutthroats and of atrocious
and semi-demoniacal bloodstained females; just as in its
subsequent modern history it found its most conspicuous
expression in Prussianism, from the Teutonic Knights to
Frederick II of Hohenzollern and to Bismarck, the founder
of unity, who gave his imprint to the new Germany with
everything he had in himself of the cruel, sneering and
cynical, an imprint which those who succeeded him incised
more strongly in its face.

Once these and other similar German historical traditions

had been fused with the romantic decadence we have out-
lined, straight out of the mixture came racism, the new zoological form of the myth of the chosen people "which does
not contaminate itself with the nations"; so that one might
almost say that the fight to the death which "Germanism"
has undertaken against "Hebraism" comes from no other
than professional jealousy and rivalry, since, as is well known,
this concept is rigorously Hebraic and was conceived and put
forward in the fourth century before Christ by Esdras, who
however had some serious motive for holding by it. All the
cynically and obscenely ferocious words we have heard with
shudders in the course of the present war issued from the
mouths of that people, boasting of its warlike destiny and
scorning its adversaries as merchants. These are the ugly
words which are fabricated in war when it is elevated to the
ideal, which by its internal logic is led to adopt sentiments,
attitudes, images and accents usual in the world of crime:
such is not the custom of the despised merchant peoples,
whose custom is sociable and preserves even in the agitation
of passion the restraint and the manners of good breeding
and moral discrimination.

It is probable and indeed natural that at the end of this
long and terribly ruinous war there will again be discussions
and excogitations on the way of establishing in the world
"perpetual peace" (whereas it would be a great enough thing
if there could be established a peace temporary but durable,
in which all the peoples might find, as near as may be, their
best); perpetual peace is perpetual utopia because it contem-
plates nothing more or less than the shattering of the main-
spring of human life, which is in sorrow and peril. But what
certainly should and can be done, facilitated by the lessons

of experience, is to clear away from the mind every residuum and tear out every smallest root or filament of "war as ideal," and against the warrior set up the worth of the citizen and merchant, being warned even in this by experience that merchants know how, when they are pulled into it by necessity, to hold their own against warriors and win, as can be seen at the present time and as our far-off ancestors of the Lombard League taught the warriors of Barbarossa. That we Italians, in spite of our ancient and recent traditions so clearly opposed to those of Germany and Prussia, should have been swept on to serve the policy animated by them, by a faction which had mastered the powers of the state and degraded to its instrumentality a king whose title came from national and liberal plebiscites, is one of the strangest and most horrible distortions that the interweaving of events can bring about in a people. Then was when we heard the solemn exhortation to make ourselves, in a word which had always been repugnant to us, "militarists": we listened to the lesson administered to us in the inspired accent of the elementary schoolmaster who has freshly received, dogmatically, in his non-critical mind, and hastens to proclaim it before the peoples, that which seems to him a profound and original scientific truth but which is altogether banality and foolishness:

"We not only do not believe in perpetual peace, but we consider it a depressant and a negation of the fundamental virtues of man, which only through the cruelty of battle are demonstrated in the light of the sun."

As if in the course of public and private life there could be any fear that sorrow and tragedy might be lacking, and with them the opportunities to prove the virtues proper to man!

But here I must stop, feeling as I do that from the theoretical clarification which I had proposed to make of certain concepts concerning historiography and ethics, I have trespassed into cases and problems of our present life, and have entered into the heart of our dolorous passion, to the appeals of which the purpose of attending solely to scientific discourse today cannot always close the gates of the soul. At all events even this trespass carries with it a proof of the importance of the rebellion that took place in the nineteenth century against histories of wars and the fecundity of the new beginning which historiography made from then onward.

Duties and duty

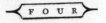
Duties and duty

WE know (or at any rate my own readers know it only too well!)[1] that the spirit is a system of distinctions which is for that reason itself a unity. If the distinctions were not, the unity would not be; since a unity without distinctions is mathematical and abstract, not organic and complete. If the unity were not, neither would the distinctions be, because they are such only in the unity which they compose, and outside of unity that noun loses all sense, becoming a simple sound of the voice. By this full identity of the two terms it is not permitted to pose unity, as often has been attempted, as the superior principle from which the distinctions separate, as it were a mythical God who, existing in himself resolves to create a world, instead of the true God who creates himself with the world and creates it enjoying and suffering. The very same activity which has the specifically unifying function is one of the distinctions, or it may be said one of the forms of the spirit, and is called moral activity, which continually conquers disharmony, that is to say the necessary

---

[1] Croce means that the philosophical ideas touched on in the opening of this essay are perhaps only too familiar to his readers, as he has stated them often over many years. They are an important part of his fundamental system. (Tr.)

negative moment of every activity, attaining spiritual harmony, thanks to which the spirit moves from conquest to conquest and life continually enlarges upon itself.

Disharmony, the negative moment, is in fact the ever resurgent desire of a particular form of the spirit to persist and develop without taking account of the other forms, from which it is necessarily born as new from old in order to become old itself, leading the others and retreading with the others the eternal spiritual circle. It is, for example, the pretense of creating poetry with a soul empty of the experience of human passions and such that it comes to conclusions within itself, as the aesthetes and decadents believe, without resonance and without consequences in the whole spirit, without producing an ulterior mental and practical process. The same may be said of philosophical thinking or of practical doing which force themselves into absolute self-sufficiency or autarchy, endeavoring, the former to do without practical, moral or poetical life, the latter to do without theoretical, moral and religious life. Not, of course, that this deviation and error has not, like all deviations and errors, a motive of truth in it, since every special form of activity obeys a law of its own and a "duty" of its own. But the deviation or error comes from wishing to rise above everything of which one is a part, contradictorily substituting the part for the whole. Thus, under the appearance of rigid observance, a duty passes over effectively into violation of duty.

Among the perils of spiritual life this is the most insidious and, it might be said, the most diabolical, if the devil (as Dante heard them say in the theological schools of Bologna) is "a liar and the father of lies." Nor is it needful nowadays to collect or multiply examples when we have had for several

years before our eyes the spectacle of a people which con-
tributed greatly in the past to the work of Europe, which,
entering into a horrible delirium, not only exalted the negative to the place of the positive, and made of war, which had
been counted for centuries as one of the three calamities
along with ~estilence and famine, an ideal of superior life,
the only one worthy of the German man, hero and warrior
by nature, but also, with equal distortion, conferred abstract
absoluteness on the concept of the fatherland and on the
duty of defending the fatherland. Love of one's country has
justification and moral worth only when it is born and lives
on the trunk of humanity, toward which it stands in one
respect as a compendious image and a symbol thereof, and,
in another respect, as the nearest field, even though certainly
not the exclusive field, of our duties. Montesquieu nobly
wrote in a notebook of his thoughts: *"Si je savais quelque
chose utile à ma patrie et qui fût préjudiciable à l'Europe, ou
bien qui fût utile à l'Europe et préjudiciable au Genre hu-
main je la regarderais comme un crime."* [1]

A fatherland which is to stand *über Alles*, if it were not
as it usually is a simple emphatical expression, would express
a perverse and criminal feeling. Similarly the war maxim
to "do the greatest damage to the enemy" encounters its
logical and moral limits in the exclusion of such damage
as strikes that which is equally sacred to the enemy and
to ourselves, that which, being lost, diminishes both him
and us, and us rather more than him, when we have been
authors of the loss and take upon ourselves the hatred and
shame. Herein is the moral momentum of what is called

---

[1] *Cahiers* (1716-55), ed. Grasset (Paris, 1942), pp. 9, 108, 241.

jus gentium, natural law or international law, which in every other respect is a law like the others. I have on my heart, as I write these words (October, 1943), the destruction which officers of the German command deliberately made in vile reprisal and, in spite of having been warned that they were about to destroy things which belonged neither to Naples nor to Italy but to the international world of studies, pitilessly carried out, of the Great Archives of Naples, with their treasures of medieval parchments, the register of Frederick II of Hohenstauffen, the Angevin registers, the Aragonese chancellery, the Farnese papers, the documents of Neapolitan history which were interwoven with those of the history of Europe and the Orient, inexhaustible fount of precious information, object of indefatigable research by Italians and foreigners, jealously preserved all down the centuries, now no longer in existence, devoured by the flames after having been sprinkled with gasoline. How many hours of my youth did I pass consulting those volumes, and those other bundles of papers, now also ashes, which contained the records of Southern commune and family life! With what joy I returned to them whenever my studies led me back again! How I see now, with eyes veiled in tears at the memory of their persons, those old men, those masters of mine, who were, in the most ancient monastery of San Severino, their proud and loving custodians—Bartolomeo Capasso at the head of them all! And to think that the man or men who, in the light of the culture of the world and of Germany, made themselves guilty of such an act, which is altogether comparable to those habitual to poor ignorant barbarians like Alaric or Genseric and suchlike *deutsche Recken*, giants of German history, can make themselves believe, perhaps, that

in this way they have served their fatherland and fulfilled
their duty!

But men who keep themselves fundamentally, substantially men know how to make duties submit to duty (as Schiller said he denied particular religions *aus Religion*, because
of religion), and spring at once, with the heart which does
not deceive, to the right side, in such emotion as sometimes
breaks out spontaneously even in the souls of brigands and
others given to sin and vice and crime, who have not burned
out in themselves every spark of humanity, and have not
fallen into the state of automata and machines, as—all too
truly—have those Germans whom we saw devastate Europe
all around us, and who today systematically and methodically
are destroying our Italy not only in the lives of her citizens,
not only in the patrimony of her sons' weary labor, but in
the ideal patrimony in which she was and is a mistress to
other peoples. Fear, repugnance and horror diffuse themselves about those men because of the extreme degradation
of humanity which has befallen them through their fatherland and devotion to the fatherland and discipline for the
fatherland, through that stupidity of an extrinsic and pedan-
tically conceived duty and of a blind, inhuman obedience to
an idol or Moloch of theirs. "Inhumanity," is the word which
rises above all others; and I still remember, by contrast, with
what accents a young Jewish lady, a student of classical an-
tiquities, who came to Italy after the ferocious persecution
of the Jews in Germany had begun, carrying in her thin face
and sorrowful eyes the signs of the shock and misery she had
suffered, said to me in wonder at the welcome she found
in Italy: "The Italians are human!"

How it came to pass that the Germans, whom we used to

love in the high thought of their classical philosophy, in their Goethe's poetry, in music and in the good fellowship of their honest and industrious customs, and still further admired for the services they rendered to science and technique, for the wealth and power to which they had raised their country, have become that which they are today, an object of abhorrence for the whole world on the part of every kind of person, is a problem harassed with terrible difficulties: it imposes itself upon the entire world for that day in which we must somehow establish a cohabitation of peoples and in which certainly we shall not dream of canceling the German people from the earth.

I have never believed, and most certainly I will not be led by passion now to believe, in the myth of peoples and races and of their indelible characters; and I shall continue to adhere to the concept, both critical and consoling, that such characters are not naturalistic and deterministic facts, but historical formations, of more or less long duration, of various intensities, which can be dissolved and give place to other different and opposite formations; and this historical formation of that which stands before us today as Germanism I have summarily traced out elsewhere for what it is. But perhaps in the conceit of superiority of the Germans toward the other peoples, in their weakness for the argument of force, in the language of the conquering barbarian which is their habit, there is, more than may seem at first, a hidden tormenting consciousness of inferiority because they have never yet succeeded in competing with the other peoples in the liveliness and clarity of intuition, in the art, style and act of behavior, in moving others to interest and sympathy and attracting the imagination and giving rise to imitation and

fashion, in calling luck to themselves and taking advantages
that are spontaneously offered, thus giving proof of political
sense; in making themselves respected by respecting others:
so that for their limitless ambition and their dream of the
Kolossal there is nothing left to try except imposition by
violence. The scourge, the club, and whatever more modern
and more scientific and more terrifying weapons have been
substituted for or added to these, have seemed means con-
ducive to procuring for them, by short cuts, the dominion of
the world, from which, obtained in this manner, in a vacuum
and what is more in the midst of the revolt of every moral
force, one cannot see how they could ever profit. "Tri-
umphs," once said a poet of theirs in the time when Germany, too, warmed itself in the rays of European liberty,
"are equal to defeats when their fruit consists in the lamenta-
tion and boundless hatred of the world." [1]

---

[1] *"Triumphe sind wie Niederlagen*
Wenn ihre Frucht besteht in Klagen
Im grenzlosen Hass der Welt."
                    —August von Platen: *Polenlieder* (1831).

An epigraph

Written at the request of Stoneman, who, having gone to visit Croce in Sorrento, told him, still deeply moved, what he had seen and learned, and declared his intention of placing a stone at his own cost in the cemetery of Caiazzo to pass on the memory of the slaughter. (B.C.)

NEAR CAIAZZO
IN THE PLACE CALLED SAN GIOVANNI E PAOLO
SOME FAMILIES OF COUNTRY PEOPLE
SHELTERED IN THE SAME HOUSE
WERE ON XXII OCTOBER MCMXLIII .
SHOT AND MACHINE-GUNNED
BY ORDER OF A YOUNG PRUSSIAN OFFICER
MEN WOMEN AND CHILDREN
TWENTY-THREE HUMBLE CREATURES
GUILTY ONLY
OF HAVING UNWITTINGLY
AT THE QUESTION
WHERE THE ENEMY WAS TO BE FOUND
INDICATED TO HIM NO OTHER THAN THE WAY
TOWARD WHICH THE GERMANS WERE TURNED
WITHOUT FORETHOUGHT
THERE ISSUED FROM THEIR LIPS
THE WORD OF TRUTH
DESIGNATING NOT THE HUMAN ADVERSARY
IN HUMAN WARS
BUT THE ATROCIOUS PRESENT ENEMY
OF HUMANITY

———

WILLIAM H. STONEMAN
AMERICAN JOURNALIST
WHO SAW WITH HORROR AND PITY
THE BODIES OF THE MURDERED
RAISES THIS MEMORIAL